W9-BLX-366

COOKING

THE

MEXICAN

WAY

This book is available in two editions:
Library binding by Lerner Publications Company,
    a division of Lerner Publishing Group
Soft cover by First Avenue Editions,
    an imprint of Lerner Publishing Group
241 First Avenue North
Minneapolis, MN 55401 U.S.A.

Website address: www.lernerbooks.com

Library of Congress Cataloging-in-Publication Data

Coronado, Rosa.
    Cooking the Mexican way / by Rosa Coronado—Rev. & expanded
    p. cm. — (Easy menu ethnic cookbooks)
    Includes index.
    ISBN 0-8225-4117-3 (lib. bdg. : alk. paper)
    ISBN 0-8225-4162-9 (pbk. : alk. paper)
    1. Cookery, Mexican—Juvenile literature. 2. Mexico—Social life and customs—Juvenile literature. [1. Cookery, Mexican. 2. Mexico—Social life and customs.] I. Title. II. Series.
TX716.M4 C67 2002
641.5′972—dc21
                                                      00-011175

Manufactured in the United States of America
2 3 4 5 6 7 – JR – 08 07 06 05 04 03

easy menu ethnic cookbooks

COOKING

THE

revised and expanded

to include new low-fat

MEXICAN

and vegetarian recipes

WAY

Rosa Coronado

Lerner Publications Company • Minneapolis

Contents

Introduction

When U.S. citizens visit Mexico, they often see only the towns just across the border, with their souvenir shops and fast-food stands. These people never get a glimpse of the real Mexico, a large, culturally rich, and complicated country that stretches for one thousand miles beyond the border it shares with the United States, its northern neighbor. And they don't get a chance to sample the goodness of authentic Mexican food.

Corn is a staple of the Mexican diet. It is often dried and ground into flour to be made into tortillas. Fried tortillas with cheese and chile strips make nachos—a great snack. (Recipe on page 55.)

UNITED STATES

Juárez

Río Grande

SIERRA MADRE OCCIDENTAL

Gulf of California

SIERRA MADRE ORIENTAL

Monterrey

MEXICO

Gulf of Mexico

Pacific Ocean

JALISCO

MICHOACÁN

Mexico City

Puebla

PUEBLA

VERACRUZ

Veracruz

YUCATÁN PENINSULA

Caribbean Sea

SIERRA MADRE DEL SUR

OAXACA

Oaxaca

GUATEMALA

The Land and the People

The thirty-one states of Mexico are spread out over a land nearly as varied in climate and geography as the rest of the world put together. Rocky deserts, misty mountains, steamy rain forests, fertile plains—all of these can be found in Mexico, often within the same small geographical region.

The lives of the Mexican people are almost as varied as the country's landscape and climate. In the large cities, many Mexicans work in modern office buildings and live in comfortable apartments, while others make their homes in crowded, low-income neighborhoods. The capital, Mexico City, is the second largest city in the world and has most of the problems that plague big cities everywhere, including traffic jams and air pollution. But outside the capital, there are smaller, less crowded communities such as Oaxaca, where the air is clean and life is less hectic. In these towns, flowers bloom on the patios of whitewashed houses, and young people often take the traditional walk around the central plaza each evening at sunset. Even farther from the bustle of the big city, Indian farmers in the states of Yucatán and Chiapas live in thatch-roofed houses and go to work each day in the cornfields, using many of the same kinds of tools that their ancestors used one thousand years ago.

One thousand years ago, the country that we call Mexico was inhabited by groups of Maya Indians, who had a very advanced civilization. They built large cities out of stone, developed systems of writing and arithmetic, and created beautiful works of art. By the time soldiers and explorers from Spain arrived in Mexico during the early 1500s, another powerful group of Indians, the Aztecs, ruled the land from a great city called Tenochtitlán, located where modern Mexico City stands. The Spaniards conquered the Aztecs, destroyed their capital city, and took possession of their land. From this harsh beginning, the modern nation of Mexico was born.

Most Mexicans are descended from both Spanish and Indian ancestors. People with this ethnic background are called mestizos, which means "people of mixed blood." Mestizos have inherited the customs and traditions of two very different civilizations, and the food of Mexico is a fascinating blend of these two rich cultures.

Mexican Heritage

The Indians of ancient Mexico ate many foods that were unknown to Europeans in the 1500s. These foods are still an important part of the Mexican diet. Among them are corn, tomatoes, squash, avocados, and many varieties of beans and peppers. Another food that ancient Mexicans gave to the world was chocolate, which had a very special meaning to the Mayas, Aztecs, and other Indian civilizations. Cacao beans—from which chocolate is made—were sometimes used as money. A bitter drink made from the beans was considered sacred and was reserved only for priests and rulers. Chocolate sweetened with sugar is popular all over the world, but the people of Mexico have a special fondness for it.

Of all the foods native to Mexico, corn is the most popular and most important, in modern times as well as in the past. The corn tortilla—a kind of thin, flat pancake—accompanies almost all Mexican meals, either as bread or as part of the main dish.

A versatile food, the tortilla can be toasted or fried, rolled or

A Mexican cook makes corn tortillas the old-fashioned way—by hand.

folded, stuffed with meats or vegetables, or topped with rich sauces. Many modern Mexican cooks make their tortillas from a specially prepared dough called *masa*, or they buy them every day from *tortillerías*, stores that sell freshly made tortillas. In some rural areas, however, tortillas are still made in the age-old way. Kernels of dried corn are cooked in lime water until soft and then are ground by hand with the mano and metate, stone grinding implements used for centuries by the Indians of Mexico. Pieces of the soft corn dough are shaped and flattened by hand until they are just the right thickness. Then they are cooked over an open fire on a clay or metal griddle called a *comal*. Tortillas made by this method are delicious, but the process takes a great deal of time. It is not surprising that modern Mexican cooks use shortcuts in preparing this important food.

Another native food essential to Mexican cooking is the *chile*, or pepper. Relatives of the familiar bell pepper, Mexican chiles come in many sizes, colors, and flavors. Some are more than twelve inches long, while others are no bigger than a dried bean. When they are young, chiles are usually various shades of green and yellow. When they become ripe, most of them turn bright red or orange. Many chiles have a sweet, mild flavor, but some are so hot that they make your eyes water just to smell them. These fabulous peppers have beautiful names such as jalapeño, poblano, and serrano. They give a special flavor to a great variety of Mexican dishes.

Mexican cooking also depends on many ingredients that are not native to the country but were brought from Europe by the early Spanish settlers. Beef, chicken, and pork are European contributions to the Mexican table. The only domestic animals used for food by the Aztecs and other Indians were wild turkeys and small, fat wild dogs. Rice and wheat also arrived with the European settlers, as did spices such as cinnamon and cloves. Because of their European heritage, modern Mexicans enjoy apples and peaches in addition to the papayas, mangoes, and other tropical fruits known to their Indian ancestors.

Holidays and Festivals

When Mexicans cook for a special occasion, they devote a great deal of energy to the meal. They plan menus that involve many elaborate dishes, each of which requires several steps to prepare. People may spend several days preparing ingredients and cooking the time-consuming, complicated recipes. Often, every family member—or even everyone in a small village—will be given a task, such as grinding chiles or shelling nuts, to help get ready for the celebration.

Most Mexicans are Roman Catholics, so the most important holidays in Mexico are Roman Catholic celebrations. Christmas is one of the biggest of these occasions. The Christmas season starts on December 16 with a tradition called *las posadas*. In each neighborhood, groups of children reenact the biblical story of Mary and Joseph's search for lodging. The children sing carols at their neighbors' doors and request to be let in for the night. The first two households refuse, but the third invites the group inside for a party. Las posadas takes place each night from December 16 through Christmas Eve (December 24), and a different neighbor hosts each evening. At each party, children break a piñata (a festive pottery or papier-mâché container filled with sweets) and scramble for the peanuts, oranges, and pieces of sugarcane that spill out.

The people of Oaxaca, a region of southern Mexico, eat fried pastries called *buñuelos* during the Christmas season. An interesting custom is associated with the snack. On Christmas Eve, street vendors sell buñuelos in the town plazas, serving them to customers on pottery dishes that have cracks or flaws in them. After eating the pastries, the people throw the dishes on the ground and break them. This custom seems to have very ancient roots and may be connected to ancient Indian ceremonies celebrating the end of the old year and the beginning of a new one.

Christmas Eve supper would not be complete without *bacalao a la vizcaína*, or Christmas Eve salt cod. This dish shows a strong Spanish influence, as most of the ingredients and the cooking method are from Spain. The salt-dried cod is soaked in water for a few days and then cooked with tomatoes, onion, garlic, almonds, olives, chiles, and parsley. Families serve the dish with bread rolls and use any leftovers as filling for snacks.

At midnight—that is, very early on Christmas morning—people go to church for the Christmas service. Then they come home to eat a festive dinner, the main course of which may be tamales. To make tamales, cooks fill pockets of corn dough with beans, meat, or other fillings, wrap the cakes in corn husks or banana leaves, and steam the tamales until the dough is cooked. Another popular Christmas dish is turkey mole. Mexico's ancient kings and nobles enjoyed this magnificent meal of turkey in a mole—a complicated sauce. In modern times, the dish is a common choice for any occasion that calls for a special meal. A mole contains many ingredients—chiles, seeds, fruits, and even a small amount of chocolate—that are cooked first by themselves, then ground and cooked together until thick. The word *mole* comes from the Spanish verb *moler*, which means "to grind." Modern moles contain spices such as cinnamon, cloves, and black pepper, all of which Spanish conquerors introduced to Mexico centuries ago.

According to Christian tradition, three kings brought gifts to the newborn Christ child on January 6, also called Three Kings' Day. On this day, Mexicans gather to exchange their Christmas presents. They eat *rosca de reyes*, a ring-shaped loaf of sweet, rich bread decorated with fruits, nuts, sugar, and preserves. A small clay or plastic doll is hidden in the loaf. Whoever finds the doll in his or her slice has to throw a party on February 2, or Candlemas—a celebration of Jesus' first visit to a temple. Another guest at the Three Kings' Day gathering may find a dried bean in the bread. He or she must bring the beverages for the Candlemas party.

Eastertime is just as important and festive as the Christmas season. A forty-day period called Lent comes before Easter Sunday. During Lent, Mexican Roman Catholics avoid rich foods and do not eat red meat. One traditional Lenten dish is *revoltijo*, a mole served with vegetables and fried shrimp cakes. To make the cakes, cooks toast and grind salty, dried shrimps, combine them with eggs and breadcrumbs, and fry dollops of the mixture.

The week before Easter Sunday is called Holy Week. It commemorates the events that Christians believe led up to Jesus' crucifixion. Worshipers attend church services on each day of Holy Week. Townsfolk take statues of Jesus and Mary from their churches, decorate the statues, and parade them around town. On Good Friday, people perform a passion play—a reenactment of the trial, crucifixion, death, and resurrection of Jesus. During Holy Week and the week following Easter, banks, government offices, and most businesses are closed. Many Mexicans take a two-week vacation during this time. For this reason, beaches and resorts are especially crowded around Easter.

September is the month of the walnut harvest and also of Mexico's Independence Day (September 16). During this month, Mexicans make a patriotic dish called *chiles en nogada,* or stuffed poblano chiles in walnut sauce. Cooks roast and peel the chiles and fill them with a meat mixture that traditionally includes a chopped peach and a chopped pear. A sauce made of peeled, ground walnuts, white cheese, and sour cream tops the chiles. The red seeds of a third fruit, the pomegranate, round out the dish. The green chiles, white sauce, and red garnish represent the three colors of Mexico's flag.

November 2 is All Souls' Day, or Día de los Muertos. People bring picnic dinners to cemeteries and eat meals at the gravesites of departed loved ones. Tradition holds that the dead enjoy these feasts, too. To celebrate the holiday, cooks bake *pan de muertos* (the bread of the dead), which are round loaves decorated with dough skulls and bones or loaves shaped like human skeletons. People also decorate their homes with paper skeletons and eat candies shaped like skulls.

In addition to these and other national holidays, Mexicans celebrate regional festivals. Every community has a patron saint—a saint who is believed to guard the town and its inhabitants. Citizens hold a celebration on the feast day of their town's patron saint. The

Decorated candy skulls are among the treats that can be found in Mexico during Día de los Muertos.

merriment usually includes fireworks, games such as bullfights or cockfights, music, dancing, and plenty of food. Snack vendors keep busy serving local specialties to hungry partygoers.

In many Mexican towns, a *feria*, or fair, celebrates the harvest of a locally important food. People serve dishes made from the special ingredient. Some of the foods celebrated in at least one Mexican town include rice, corn, pineapple, vanilla, coffee, amaranth (a grain grown in Mexico for thousands of years), and nopales (a cactus that Mexicans serve as a vegetable).

Beautiful red chiles are for sale in Mexican markets.

At the Mercado

When Mexican cooks shop for the fruits, meats, and vegetables needed for the dishes on their menus, they often go to an open-air *mercado*, or market. Busy markets can be found in the villages and towns of the Mexican countryside as well as in big cities like Guadalajara and Mexico City. Shoppers make a selection from a tempting variety of fruits and vegetables arranged in neat piles in stands or on the ground. There are dark green avocados and bright green limes, golden yellow papayas, rich red tomatoes, and chiles in all shades of green, yellow, and red. In another part of the market are bags full of dried corn. Baskets are heaped with dark red beans, pale pink beans, and beans spotted like a pinto pony. The air is heavy with the fragrance of ripe fruit and the sharp smell of green herbs such as cilantro, or fresh coriander—a popular seasoning. Shoppers quietly bargain over prices and fill their net bags with purchases that will become part of the day's meals.

Markets like these have existed in Mexico for centuries, and they are still an important part of Mexican life. In many cities, there are *supermercados* (supermarkets) where canned and frozen foods can be obtained, but many Mexican cooks make a daily trip to an outdoor market to buy fresh fruits and vegetables. Homes in rural areas of Mexico often have no refrigeration, so food cannot be stored for very long. Even when storage is possible, many Mexican cooks believe that food tastes best when it is prepared fresh every day.

U.S. citizens who want to cook Mexican food can sometimes go to an outdoor market to buy fresh chiles. They can also get most of the ingredients they need at local grocery stores and supermarkets. In parts of the United States with large Mexican American populations, there are stores that sell special ingredients such as dried chiles and Mexican chocolate. If you are lucky enough to live in such an area, you can get just about anything you need for a Mexican menu, including stacks of warm, freshly made tortillas. Whether you get your tortillas from a tortillería or from the dairy case at the corner supermarket, you should give Mexican cooking a try. The recipes in this book are easy to prepare and will give you a true taste of Mexican food.

Before You Begin

Cooking any dish, plain or fancy, is easier and more fun if you are familiar with the ingredients. Mexican cooking makes use of some ingredients that you may not know. Sometimes special cookware is used, too, although the recipes in this book can easily be prepared with ordinary utensils and pans.

Before you start cooking, read "The Careful Cook" and carefully study the following "dictionary" of special ingredients and terms. Next, read through the recipe you want to try from beginning to end. Then you will be ready to shop for ingredients and to organize the cookware you will need. Once you have assembled everything, you can begin to cook.

Ensalada de frijoles *(recipe on page 58)* uses several ingredients native to Mexico.

The Careful Cook

Whenever you cook, there are certain safety rules you must always keep in mind. Even experienced cooks follow these rules when they are in the kitchen.

- Always wash your hands before handling food. Thoroughly wash all raw vegetables and fruits to remove dirt, chemicals, and insecticides. Wash uncooked poultry, fish, and meat under cold water.
- Use a cutting board when cutting up vegetables and fruits. Don't cut them up in your hand! And be sure to cut in a direction *away* from you and your fingers.
- Long hair or loose clothing can easily catch fire if brought near the burners of a stove. If you have long hair, tie it back before you start cooking.
- Turn all pot handles toward the back of the stove so that you will not catch your sleeves or jewelry on them. This is especially important when younger brothers and sisters are around. They could easily knock off a pot and get burned.
- Always use a pot holder to steady hot pots or to take pans out of the oven. Don't use a wet cloth on a hot pan because the steam it produces could burn you.
- Lift the lid of a steaming pot with the opening away from you so that you will not get burned.
- If you get burned, hold the burn under cold running water. Do not put grease or butter on it. Cold water helps to take the heat out, but grease or butter will only keep it in.
- If grease or cooking oil catches fire, throw baking soda or salt at the bottom of the flame to put it out. (Water will *not* put out a grease fire.) Call for help, and try to turn all the stove burners to "off."

Cooking Utensils

fat thermometer—A special thermometer used for testing the temperature of hot fat for frying

molinillo—A special wooden beater with rings of different sizes on it. It can be obtained in shops that specialize in Mexican goods.

tongs—A utensil used to grasp food. Tongs are commonly shaped either like tweezers or scissors, with flat, blunt ends.

Cooking Terms

blend—To combine ingredients, usually in a blender or food processor, until smooth

boil—To heat a liquid over high heat until bubbles form and rise rapidly to the surface

brown—To cook food quickly in fat over high heat so that the surface turns an even brown

fry—To cook quickly in hot fat

grate—To cut food into tiny pieces by rubbing it against a grater

knead—To work dough by pressing it with the palms, pushing it outward, and then pressing it over on itself

preheat—To allow an oven to warm up to a certain temperature before putting food in it

sauté—To fry quickly in oil or fat over high heat, stirring or turning the food to prevent burning

shred—To tear or cut into small pieces, either by hand or with a grater

simmer—To cook over low heat in liquid kept just below its boiling point. Bubbles may occasionally rise to the surface.

Special Ingredients

avocado—A fruit native to Mexico, which also can be found in most parts of the United States, with pulpy, edible flesh. Avocados are ripe if they feel slightly soft when gently sqeezed. If you buy an unripe avocado, let it sit unrefrigerated for a few days to ripen.

basil—A rich and fragrant herb whose leaves are used in cooking. It is also sold in dried form in the spice section of supermarkets.

CHILE PEPPERS

green chile—One of the milder hot peppers, about two inches in length

jalapeño—A spicy green pepper that can be bought canned or fresh

poblano—A large, dark-green pepper that is triangular in shape. Poblano peppers are sometimes labeled *pasilla* in fresh produce bins.

serrano—A hot pepper, green or red in color, that is slightly smaller and thinner than a jalapeño

chili powder—A mixture of ground chiles and other herbs and spices, including cumin and oregano

cumin—An aromatic spice used to flavor foods. Cumin seeds can be used whole or, more commonly, in a powdered form made by grinding the seeds.

garlic—An herb whose distinctive flavor is used in many dishes. Fresh garlic can usually be found in the produce department of a supermarket. Each piece, or bulb, can be broken up into several small sections called cloves. Most recipes use only one or two finely chopped cloves of this very strong herb. Before you chop up a clove of garlic, you will have to peel off the brittle, papery covering that surrounds it.

kidney bean—A large kidney-shaped bean. You can buy kidney beans dried or in cans.

lard—A solid shortening made from pork fat. Vegetable shortening can be substituted for lard.

mango—A tropical fruit with a thin, green-orange skin and sweet, peachy-orange flesh. At the center of a mango is a hard seed, or pit.

masa harina—Special Mexican tortilla flour that is mixed with water to make a soft dough. Masa harina is available at most specialty groceries and some supermarkets.

Mexican chocolate—Used primarily to make the beverage hot chocolate, Mexican chocolate is sold in small tablets flavored with sugar, cinnamon, and other ingredients. Many specialty groceries and supermarkets carry Mexican chocolate.

mole—A thick, spicy sauce made with chiles, seeds, spices, and usually chocolate and served with meat. Mole can vary from cook to cook. It is used in many traditional Mexican festival dishes. Jars of prepared mole paste can be purchased in the United States at most specialty stores and in many supermarkets.

oregano—The dried leaves, whole or powdered, of a rich and fragrant herb that is used as a seasoning in cooking

pimentos—Small, sweet red chiles that come in cans or bottles and are often used to add color to food

pinto bean—A spotted red bean that has a soft, smooth texture when cooked. The pinto bean gets its name from its appearance—*pinto* is the Spanish word for "spotted."

sweetened condensed milk—A mixture of whole milk and sugar that has been thickened by evaporating most of the water from the mixture

tortillas—Round, flat, very thin pancakes made of corn or wheat flour used commonly in Mexican cooking. Crisp-fried tortillas are used for tacos and tostadas.

vermicelli noodles—Long, very thin pasta sometimes used in Mexican soups

Healthy and Low-Fat Cooking Tips

The Mexican food at U.S. restaurants is often loaded with fat. Many popular dishes that U.S. cooks prepare at home are high in fat as well. But authentic Mexican cooking doesn't need to be high-fat to be tasty. You can modify recipes and cooking methods to cut or eliminate fat.

Did you know that salsa, a favorite Mexican condiment, has no fat at all? Mexicans serve many different kinds of salsa to add flavor to almost any food. Offer it alongside tacos and other snacks or slather it over main dishes just before serving for a burst of color and taste.

Several recipes in this book call for frying some of the ingredients. Frying typically adds fat to a dish. Cooks can reduce this fat by frying in a smaller amount of oil or in a nonstick skillet with cooking spray instead of oil. Instead of frying tortillas for some dishes, toast them in the oven at 325°F or in a dry frying pan until crisp.

Many traditional Mexican ingredients, such as meat, cheese, and sour cream, are high in fat. In Mexico's countryside, these foods may be expensive, and people may not eat them every day. Families skip these ingredients or reduce the amounts when cooking everyday meals. U.S. cooks can do the same. In addition, you can use lower-fat substitutes. Turkey, tofu, and fish are all much lower in fat than beef or pork. Cottage cheese or plain yogurt, drained in a strainer lined with cheesecloth, both make good substitutes for sour cream.

Lard is an important ingredient in many Mexican dishes, but it is high in saturated fat and cholesterol. Medical research has shown that a diet high in these two kinds of fat can lead to heart disease. Health-conscious cooks may want to substitute vegetable shortening, canola oil, or olive oil for lard. (These ingredients have the same amount of total fat but a much lower proportion of saturated fat and no cholesterol.) Some dishes may look or taste a litte bit different as a result, but they will still be delicious.

METRIC CONVERSIONS

Cooks in the United States measure both liquid and solid ingredients using standard containers based on the 8-ounce cup and the tablespoon. These measurements are based on volume, while the metric system of measurement is based on both weight (for solids) and volume (for liquids). To convert from U.S. fluid tablespoons, ounces, quarts, and so forth to metric liters is a straightforward conversion, using the chart below. However, since solids have different weights—one cup of rice does not weigh the same as one cup of grated cheese, for example—many cooks who use the metric system have kitchen scales to weigh different ingredients. The chart below will give you a good starting point for basic conversions to the metric system.

MASS (weight)

1 ounce (oz.)	=	28.0 grams (g)
8 ounces	=	227.0 grams
1 pound (lb.) or 16 ounces	=	0.45 kilograms (kg)
2.2 pounds	=	1.0 kilogram

LIQUID VOLUME

1 teaspoon (tsp.)	=	5.0 milliliters (ml)
1 tablespoon (tbsp.)	=	15.0 milliliters
1 fluid ounce (oz.)	=	30.0 milliliters
1 cup (c.)	=	240 milliliters
1 pint (pt.)	=	480 milliliters
1 quart (qt.)	=	0.95 liters (l)
1 gallon (gal.)	=	3.80 liters

LENGTH

¼ inch (in.)	=	0.6 centimeters (cm)
½ inch	=	1.25 centimeters
1 inch	=	2.5 centimeters

TEMPERATURE

212°F	=	100°C (boiling point of water)
225°F	=	110°C
250°F	=	120°C
275°F	=	135°C
300°F	=	150°C
325°F	=	160°C
350°F	=	180°C
375°F	=	190°C
400°F	=	200°C

(To convert temperature in Fahrenheit to Celsius, subtract 32 and multiply by .56)

PAN SIZES

8-inch cake pan	= 20 x 4-centimeter cake pan
9-inch cake pan	= 23 x 3.5-centimeter cake pan
11 x 7-inch baking pan	= 28 x 18-centimeter baking pan
13 x 9-inch baking pan	= 32.5 x 23-centimeter baking pan
9 x 5-inch loaf pan	= 23 x 13-centimeter loaf pan
2-quart casserole	= 2-liter casserole

A Mexican Table

Gathering around the table for a meal has always been a central part of Mexican culture and social life. Not only is mealtime a great way to share delicious food with family and friends, it is also a means by which families carry on traditions and customs that are important to their heritage.

Many of the tasty dishes served up in Mexican homes are made from recipes that have been handed down from generation to generation. Mexican cooks are proud of their specialties and make sure to pass them on to other members of the family. In rural areas, fresh ingredients such as vegetables, fruits, herbs, and chiles may come right from the family's own garden or orchard. This close connection to the land and the production of food is another Mexican tradition.

Perhaps most importantly, mealtimes are a chance for Mexican families to spend time together in the middle of a busy day. After the main meal of the day, a popular and long-standing custom is the *sobremesa*. Literally meaning "over the table," the sobremesa is a time to relax, share stories, tell jokes, and just enjoy the good company of family and friends.

Farmers harvest crisp lettuce. Fresh produce plays a central role in Mexcian cooking.

A Mexican Menu

Below is a simplified menu plan for a typical day of Mexican cooking. Two alternate dinner ideas are included.

DINNER #1

Vermicelli soup

Refried beans

Red snapper with lime juice or Zucchini and corn

Tortillas

Fresh fruit

SHOPPING LIST:

Produce

2 onions
2 limes
3 medium zucchini
1 small tomato
fresh fruit

Dairy/Egg/Meat

Monterey Jack cheese
cheddar cheese
lard or butter
6 red snapper fillets

Canned/Bottled/Boxed

vermicelli noodles
small can tomato purée
3 15-oz. cans beef or
    vegetable broth
2 c. dried pinto beans
1 can corn or 1 package
    frozen corn
tortillas

Miscellaneous

vegetable oil
flour
salt
pepper

DINNER #2

Avocado dip with
tortilla chips

Mexican rice

Tortillas with
chicken

Green salad

Mango with
cinnamon

SHOPPING LIST:

Produce

5 onions
garlic
2 to 4 poblano peppers
2 green bell peppers
2 to 3 mangoes or a 1-lb.
  can of mangoes
2 large avocados
3 tomatoes
1 to 3 serrano or jalapeño
  peppers
lettuce for salad
lime or lemon juice

Dairy/Egg/Meat

1 small container sour cream
  or plain yogurt
2 chicken breasts*
10 oz. Monterey Jack cheese
1 stick butter or margarine

Canned/Bottled/Boxed

2 16-oz. cans tomato purée
2 15-oz. cans chicken broth
1 qt. (4 c.) tomato juice
shredded coconut
tortilla chips
salad dressing
white rice
1 8-oz. can whole tomatoes

Miscellaneous

8 7-inch tortillas
vegetable oil
chili powder
ground cumin
oregano
basil
cinnamon
salt
pepper

*To make a vegetarian meal, skip the chicken
and broth in the shopping list. Instead, fill
tortillas with refried beans.

Breakfast/El Desayuno

Rural and urban Mexicans differ in their breakfast-eating habits. Country people rise very early so they can work in the fields. When they first get up at about 5 A.M., they might have a sweet roll and either *café con leche* (coffee mixed with hot milk), hot chocolate, or a hot cornmeal drink called *atole*. City people eat a similar meal, but they eat between 7 and 9 A.M. In the country, 9 A.M. is the time for a second breakfast, which is much heartier than the first. Fruit or fruit juice, eggs, beans, chile sauce, tortillas, and café con leche may be served. This meal is called *almuerzo*. Those people in the city who have only breakfasted on a cup of coffee are also likely to eat almuerzo, but they eat it much later than the country people. A city almuerzo is a meal eaten closer to the time of a U.S. lunch, at 11 or 11:30 A.M. Because many people in Mexico don't like eating early, however, this meal is not called an early lunch, but rather a late breakfast.

Hours after an early breakfast of coffee or chocolate mexicano (recipe on page 32), Mexicans gather for a heartier meal.

Mexican Hot Chocolate/*Chocolate Mexicano*

Stores that sell Mexican foods usually carry a special form of chocolate used to make this delicious chocolate drink. It comes in cakes or tablets and contains sugar and cinnamon. If you can't get this special chocolate, sweetened cooking chocolate can be used instead.

In Mexico, hot chocolate is customarily served in a large earthenware jug. It is placed on the table, where the chocolate is whipped into a froth with a wooden beater called a molinillo. If you can't find one in your neighborhood, a handheld eggbeater will work just as well.

2 3-oz. cakes or tablets of Mexican chocolate*

6 c. milk

1. Combine all ingredients in a saucepan and cook over low heat. Stir constantly until chocolate has melted and mixture is blended.

2. With a molinillo or eggbeater, beat chocolate to a froth just before serving.

Cooking time: 15 minutes

Serves 4

*If you can't find Mexican chocolate, you can use 6 oz. of semisweet baking chocolate plus 1½ tsp. cinnamon.

A steaming mug of Mexican hot chocolate is a tasty treat for any time of day.

Dinner/La Comida

Mexicans in both the city and the country generally eat their main meal in the middle of the day, sometime between 2 and 5:30 P.M. Rural people often eat stew, beans, and tortillas. Wealthier people in the city may have four or five courses—soup, rice or noodles, a main course of meat or fish, vegetables, and dessert.

The tradition of eating a big meal in the afternoon is part of Mexico's Spanish heritage. Mexicans say it is also a habit that promotes good health. People who live in the mountainous areas of Mexico believe that the high altitude tends to slow digestion. In 7,600-foot-high Mexico City, it makes sense to eat a big meal in the afternoon rather than in the evening before bedtime. But the customs of modern life have interfered with this traditional eating habit. Mexicans who work in offices and factories often don't have time for a big meal during the day. So they eat a light lunch at noon and a bigger meal in the evening.

Many Mexican dishes contain fillings of meat, beans, cheese, or vegetables. Any of these fillings can be used interchangeably. Beef or pork usually go into meals prepared for special occasions. Beans, chicken, vegetables, or even leftovers, are more everyday fare.

Spicy, savory enchiladas con pollo *(recipe on page 38) make for a satisfying meal.*

Vermicelli Soup / *Sopa de Fideos*

Fideos *is the Spanish name for vermicelli, thin noodles often used in Italian cooking.*

2 tsp. vegetable oil

½ c. vermicelli noodles, uncooked and broken into small pieces

½ c. finely chopped onion

3 tbsp. tomato purée

2½ 15-oz. cans (about 5 c.) beef or vegetable broth

½ c. grated Monterey Jack cheese or white cheddar cheese

1. Heat oil in a skillet over medium heat. Add noodles, fry until light brown, then remove.

2. In the same oil, sauté onion until soft. Add tomato purée and cook for 2 to 3 minutes, stirring constantly.

3. Combine noodles, broth, and purée in a large pan and simmer until noodles are tender (6 to 8 minutes). Add salt and pepper to taste.

4. Sprinkle with cheese and serve.

Cooking time: 25 to 30 minutes
Serves 4

Easy to make, sopa de fideos *can warm you up on a chilly day. Try it with a side of* calabacitas y elote *(recipe on page 50).*

Tortillas with Chicken/Enchiladas con Pollo

Enchiladas are one of the most versatile foods on the Mexican menu. These filled and rolled tortillas can be made in many different ways. The filling can be meat, cheese, vegetables, or any combination of these ingredients. You can top enchiladas with a canned tomato-and-chili sauce, or you can make your own sauce out of red or green tomatoes.*

The recipe given here is for enchiladas filled with chicken and cheese, plus a few other good things. The basic directions for preparing and cooking the tortillas can be used with any filling, so why not try some other combinations? How about steamed vegetables? Or browned ground beef and refried beans? Or baked fish?

Enchilada sauce:

1 medium-sized onion, finely
   chopped

2 tsp. vegetable oil

3½ c. tomato purée

2 cloves garlic, finely chopped

4 tbsp. chili powder

½ tsp. ground cumin

¼ tsp. oregano

1 tsp. salt

1. Sauté onion in oil until it is soft and yellow. Add tomato purée and garlic.

2. Gradually stir in chili powder, cumin, oregano, and salt.

3. Cover and simmer about 30 minutes, stirring frequently.

Cooking time: 35 to 40 minutes
Makes about 3 cups

*To top your enchiladas, use
3 10-oz. cans or jars of enchilada sauce
(mild or hot), heated. If you would like to
make your own enchilada sauce, use
the recipe provided.

Filling:

1 recipe Shredded Chicken Filling (page 40)

2 tsp. vegetable oil

1 large onion, chopped

1 large green bell pepper, cleaned out and chopped

½ tsp. oregano

½ tsp. basil

To make the enchiladas:

8 7-inch corn tortillas

heated enchilada sauce

2 c. filling

10 oz. Monterey Jack cheese, grated (2½ c. when grated)

sour cream or plain yogurt

You can also heat the tortilla in a microwave oven for 15 seconds to soften.

1. Heat oil in a frying pan. Sauté onion, green pepper, oregano, and basil until onion and pepper are soft.

2. Stir in the shredded chicken and heat through.

Cooking time: 15 to 20 minutes
Makes filling for 8 tortillas

1. Place a tortilla in a dry skillet and heat both sides until it softens.*

2. Remove tortilla with tongs and dip in heated enchilada sauce until tortilla is well coated.

3. Place the tortilla on a cutting board and put ¼ c. of filling in the center and sprinkle with cheese (about ¼ c.). Roll up and put in a baking pan with the opening face down. Repeat steps 1 through 3 with remaining tortillas.

4. When all tortillas have been placed in the pan, cover them with remaining sauce. Cook in a 350°F oven until sauce is bubbly (about 15 to 20 minutes).

5. Serve each enchilada with a spoonful of cold sour cream or plain yogurt and garnish with shredded cheese.

Preparation time: 15 minutes
Cooking time: 15 to 20 minutes
Serves 4

Shredded Chicken Filling/ *Pollo Picado*

Fill tacos (page 54) with plain pollo picado, *or use it to make the enchilada recipe on page 38.*

2 cans (4 c.) chicken broth

2 chicken breasts

1. In a large saucepan, heat the chicken broth to boiling.

2. Add the chicken breasts and wait until the broth boils again. Turn down the heat, cover the pan, and simmer until the meat is cooked through, about 15 to 20 minutes. If the chicken has bones, allow an extra 5 to 10 minutes.

3. Take the pan off the heat and allow the chicken to cool in the broth.

4. When the meat is cool, remove it from the broth. Use your fingers to shred the meat into bite-sized pieces. Discard any skin and bones. Save the broth for another recipe.

Cooking time: 40 to 45 minutes
Makes about 2 cups

Refried Beans/*Frijoles Refritos*

Refried beans are served at almost every meal in Mexico. The beans are not really fried twice, as the name suggests, but they are usually cooked or heated twice. Mexicans often make large batches of beans and then reheat them during the week as needed, adding a little more lard each time. Refried beans work well as a side dish or as a filling for enchiladas (page 38) or tacos (page 54).

2 c. dried pinto beans

10 c. plus 5 c. water

1 large onion, chopped

½ c. lard, butter, or bacon fat*

1 tsp. salt

*Make refried beans a healthier dish by skipping the lard, which adds flavor but also fat.

1. Wash beans thoroughly under cold running water. Remove any pebbles or stones. Put beans in a large pot containing 10 c. water and soak them for 6 to 8 hours.

2. Drain beans, rinse them, and place them in a large kettle with 5 c. fresh water and the onion.

3. Cook over medium-high heat for 1 hour or until beans are soft.

4. Add lard and salt and mash with a potato masher until all fat has melted and beans are smooth.

5. Lower heat and continue to cook beans, stirring occasionally, for about 2½ hours or until bean mixture is thick and heavy.

Soaking time: 6 to 8 hours
Cooking time: 3½ hours
Serves 8

Red Snapper with Lime Juice/
Huachinango con Jugos de Limas

Huachinango is an *Aztec* name for "red snapper," an ocean fish caught off the shores of tropical Veracruz, a Mexican state located on the Gulf of Mexico. If you visit the fish market in the busy seaport of Veracruz, you will see stands full of freshly caught snapper with shiny scales in all shades of red, pink, and yellow. This fish is also available fresh or frozen in many parts of the United States. If it is too expensive or unavailable at your grocery store, a different kind of white fish—such as haddock—may be substituted.

There are many popular Mexican recipes using red snapper, but one of the tastiest ways to fix this fish is simply to panfry it and then squeeze on fresh lime juice. Limes are more widely used in Mexican cooking than lemons. Their tangy juice gives a special flavor to fish and to fresh fruits such as papaya and mango.

6 red snapper fillets

½ c. all-purpose flour seasoned with
   salt and pepper to taste

4 tbsp. vegetable oil

2 limes, cut into wedges

1. In a shallow bowl or pie pan, mix flour with a bit of salt and pepper. Place 1 fillet in the flour mixture and turn until both sides are lightly coated. Repeat with the other fillets. Set aside on a plate.

2. Heat oil in a skillet and sauté fillets, 1 or 2 at a time, for about 5 minutes or until they are golden brown. Turn and sauté on other side.*

3. Serve with lime wedges.

Cooking time: 10 to 15 minutes
Serves 6

*To cut back on fat, place fried fish on
a plate covered with a few layers of paper towels
to absorb the oil. Or skip the oil. Wrap the fish in
a piece of aluminum foil, place the package on a
cookie sheet, and bake at 450°F for 10 to 15
minutes or until cooked through.

Mango with Cinnamon / *Mango Canela*

Mango canela is a flavorful and refreshing treat. Topping mango with coconut and cinnamon makes for a tropical dessert.

2 to 3 fresh mangoes or a 1-lb. can
  of mangoes

¼ c. shredded coconut

1 tsp. cinnamon

1. If using fresh mangoes, allow ½ mango per person. To cut up a fresh mango, place the fruit on a cutting board. Slice down each side of the mango, close to the large, flat seed in the center. You will have 2 rounded sections of fruit and 1 flat section with the seed. Place a round section on a cutting board, cut side up. Slicing down to the skin but not through it, make cuts across the mango section about every half inch. Turn the fruit 90 degrees and make another set of cuts. Hold the mango section in both hands. Push on the skin with your fingers and turn the section inside out. The flesh will separate on the cuts you made, and you will be able to pick or slice mango cubes off the skin. Repeat with the other side. Next, peel the middle section. Carefully slice the flesh from the seed.

2. Chill mangoes overnight in the refrigerator.

3. To serve, place mango in a dessert dish or fruit cup. Top with coconut and sprinkle lightly with cinnamon.

Preparation time: 15 minutes plus overnight refrigeration
Serves 4 to 6

Avocado Dip/ *Guacamole*

In the United States, this avocado mixture is usually served as a dip, but in Mexico it has many other uses. Guacamole makes a good topping for tacos or tostadas and can be served as a refreshing salad all by itself.

There are many ways to make this popular food, and all of them are delicious. The essential ingredients are avocados and lime or lemon juice. Without the acid from the fruit juice, the avocados quickly turn brown, so be sure to add it. The number of chiles you use depends on how hot you want your guacamole. Taste it before adding too many. Instead of chiles, you can use a dash of chili powder or Tabasco sauce for a little heat.

2 large (or 4 small) ripe avocados*

I small tomato, chopped

½ small onion, chopped

I to 3 jalapeño or serrano chiles, chopped

I tbsp. lime or lemon juice (fresh-squeezed is best)

¾ tsp. salt

pepper to taste

1. Cut avocados in half lengthwise, slicing to and around the center pits. Ask an adult to help you pry out pits with the point of a knife. Scoop the flesh out of the shells with a large spoon.

2. Mash avocados with a fork or potato masher and stir in other ingredients. For a very smooth mixture, combine ingredients in a blender or food processor.

3. Serve with tortilla chips or raw vegetables.

Preparation time: 15 minutes
Makes about 2 cups

Avocados are high in unsaturated fat. But unlike meat and dairy products, they have no cholesterol and are low in saturated fat.

Mexican Rice/Arroz Mexicano

Mexican rice belongs to an unusual category of Mexican dishes called sopas secas, or "dry soups." To make a sopa seca, slowly cook a starchy food such as rice, noodles, or cut-up tortillas in a soup broth. Eventually all the broth is absorbed by the starch, leaving "dry" soup. Dry soups are served as a separate course before the meat course.

1 c. uncooked white rice

4 c. tomato juice

1 tbsp. vegetable oil

4 tbsp. butter or margarine

½ tsp. ground cumin

1 tsp. salt

½ green bell pepper, cleaned out and chopped

2 garlic cloves, finely chopped

1½ c. chopped onion

2 large tomatoes, chopped, or 1 8-oz. can whole tomatoes, cut up with a spoon

1. Rinse and drain rice. Dry on paper towels.

2. In a saucepan, heat tomato juice.

3. While the juice heats, heat oil in a large frying pan and fry raw rice over medium heat, stirring constantly, until it turns light brown (about 10 to 15 minutes).

4. Add the tomato juice to the rice in the frying pan. Add the rest of the ingredients, cover, and cook over low heat until tomato juice is absorbed and rice is soft (about 20 minutes).

Cooking time: 35 to 40 minutes
Serves 4 to 6

A traditional Mexican meal isn't complete without arroz mexicano.

Zucchini and Corn / *Calabacitas y Elote*

3 medium-sized zucchini

½ c. canned or frozen corn, cooked

salt and pepper to taste

1 small tomato, cut into quarters

¼ c. grated cheddar cheese

1. Wash zucchini and cut into ½-inch cubes.

2. Place zucchini in a saucepan with corn, salt, pepper, and tomato.

3. Cover the saucepan and simmer about 8 minutes, or until zucchini is tender. (Do not add any water. Juices from the zucchini and tomato will provide enough liquid for cooking.)

4. Top with grated cheese.

Preparation time: 15 minues
Serves 4

Packed with vitamins, calabacitas y elote is a healthy and colorful dish that would complement any meal.

Snacks / Botanas

Botanas, or snacks, are a traditional—and tasty—part of Mexican cuisine. After the large and leisurely midday meal, many people don't have another real sit-down meal. Instead, they enjoy an assortment of botanas during the afternoon or early evening. Friends gather to munch on these delicious morsels in restaurants and cafés or around vendors' carts in local streets and plazas. Botanas may also be served with beverages as appetizers before a meal or at parties and celebrations. *Antojitos*, literally meaning "little whims," is another name for the variety of snacks that can be purchased from street vendors and that often serve as a substitute for an evening meal.

Botanas and antojitos vary from region to region, and each area has its specialties and favorites. Some dishes, such as tamales and tacos, are familiar even to visitors. Various dips, fruits, and nuts are popular all over Mexico. Coastal regions often incorporate seafood into their snacks, while inland regions rely more heavily on beef, pork, and beans. Whatever the local ingredients, the result is always a treat—the perfect little snack to satisfy an afternoon craving.

Tacos are a popular and versatile treat. (Recipe on page 54.)

Tacos

The word taco actually means "snack" in Spanish, but this word is used for one dish in particular. A taco is a sandwichlike snack made with tortillas, a meat or bean filling, garnish, and spicy sauce. You may find taco shells, or folded and fried tortillas, in U.S. supermarkets, but you won't find them in Mexico. Mexicans do sometimes fry tacos, filling and all, and then eat the snacks while still hot.

6 7-inch corn tortillas

1¼ c. filling, such as shredded chicken (page 40) or refried beans (page 41)

shredded lettuce

chopped tomatoes

grated Monterey Jack cheese

bottled salsa or homemade *salsa cruda* (see recipe on page 55)

1. Place about 3 tbsp. of filling and desired garnishes (lettuce, tomatoes, and cheese) on each tortilla.* Pass sauce so that everyone can help themselves.

2. To eat the taco, fold the tortilla over the filling and pick the bundle up with your fingers.

Preparation time: 15 minutes
Serves 6

*Green and red peppers, pimentos, onions, and kidney beans are delicious additions to any kind of taco.

Salsa Cruda

If you would like homemade salsa for your tacos, try this simple one made of fresh tomatoes and green chiles. Called salsa cruda (raw sauce), this spicy mixture can usually be found on all Mexican tables. It makes a good addition to almost any Mexican dish.

6 medium-sized tomatoes, finely chopped

½ c. finely chopped jalapeño or serrano chiles

⅓ c. finely chopped onion

1 tsp. salt

1. Mix all ingredients together in a bowl. Cover and refrigerate overnight to allow flavors to blend.

Preparation time: 10 minutes plus overnight refrigeration
Makes about 2 cups

Nachos

Nachos are crisp, tasty snacks made with fried corn tortillas.

2 7-inch corn tortillas cut into 6 to 8 triangles

½ c. vegetable oil

1 c. grated cheddar cheese

1. Heat oil in a frying pan. Drop in tortilla sections and fry until golden brown.

2. Using tongs, remove sections and drain on a paper towel. Let cool.

3. Preheat the oven to 250°F.

4. When tortillas are cool, place them on a cookie sheet and sprinkle with grated cheese.

5. Bake until cheese is melted (about 5 to 10 minutes).

Preparation time: 20 to 25 minutes
Serves 6 to 8

Supper / La Cena

Traditionally, Mexicans eat a very light meal at night. The everyday evening meal, called *la merienda*, is served in the early evening, around 6 or 7 P.M. At this meal, many Mexicans have only café con leche or hot chocolate and sweet rolls. Sometimes la merienda is more like the kind of meal served at teatime in England. On these occasions, people might eat tortillas, beans, or perhaps some cold meat in addition to coffee and hot chocolate.

A more formal supper served later in the evening is called *la cena*. It is still a very light meal but more special than the merienda. Mexicans might have this kind of meal when guests are invited or when there is a birthday to celebrate. La cena is eaten anytime after 8 P.M. and often as late as midnight.

Tostadas con carne (recipe on page 59) are fun to serve at parties. Everyone can choose his or her own toppings. Be creative.

Kidney Bean Salad/Ensalada de Frijoles

3 tbsp. olive or vegetable oil

1½ tbsp. vinegar

1 garlic clove, finely chopped

⅛ tsp. chili powder

½ tsp. oregano

1 16-oz. can (2 c.) kidney beans, drained

1 green pepper, cleaned out and chopped

½ c. chopped red onion

1 tbsp. chopped pimento

12 pitted black olives, sliced

½ head lettuce

1. Put oil, vinegar, garlic, chili powder, and oregano in a small jar with a tight lid. Shake vigorously.

2. In a large bowl, mix the other ingredients (except lettuce) with oil mixture.

3. Chill 2 hours or more in the refrigerator.

4. Arrange lettuce leaves on a plate and spoon salad on top.

Preparation time: 2 hours
Serves 4

Crisp Tortillas with Beef/ *Tostadas con Carne*

For a variation of this recipe, eliminate the beef or replace it with sliced pork, chicken, shrimp, or cooked vegetables.

½ c. vegetable oil

12 7-inch corn tortillas

1 lb. ground beef

½ c. chopped onion

1 10-oz. can green chiles and
    tomatoes

½ tsp. garlic salt

½ tsp. oregano

½ tsp. ground cumin

¼ tsp. chili powder

¼ tsp. basil

1 15-oz. can (about 2 c.) refried
    beans or 2 c. homemade refried
    beans (see recipe on page 41)

2 c. shredded lettuce

2 tomatoes, chopped or sliced

1 c. grated cheddar cheese

taco sauce or salsa cruda (see
    recipe on page 55)

1. Heat oil in a frying pan. Using tongs, submerge tortillas, one or two at a time, in hot oil and fry until each is crisp. Drain on a paper towel.

2. Cook beef and onion in a skillet until meat is brown.

3. Drain off excess fat from meat and onions. Stir in the can of chiles and tomatoes, garlic salt, oregano, cumin, chili powder, and basil.

4. Simmer, uncovered, for 15 minutes.

5. Heat refried beans.

6. Spread each tortilla with warm beans and then cover beans with 2 heaping tbsp. of meat mixture.

7. Top with lettuce, tomato, and cheese. Pour on taco sauce or salsa cruda to taste.

Preparation time: 45 minutes to 1 hour
Serves 6

Rice with Milk/ Arroz con Leche

This rice pudding is quite sweet, which is just the way Mexicans like it. If you prefer less sweetness, use ½ cup condensed milk with ½ cup regular milk.

½ c. white rice, uncooked

½ cinnamon stick

1½ c. water

1 c. sweetened condensed milk

2½ tbsp. raisins

cinnamon for garnish

1. Put rice, cinnamon stick, and water in a saucepan. Bring to a boil quickly. Reduce heat, cover, and simmer until water is absorbed (about 15 to 20 minutes).

2. Add milk and raisins. Cook, uncovered, until milk is absorbed into rice (10 to 15 minutes).

3. Remove from heat, take out cinnamon stick, and cover. Let sit for a few minutes. Sprinkle with cinnamon.

4. Serve rice hot or cold.

Preparation time: 40 to 45 minutes
Serves 4

Rice, cinnamon, and plump raisins combine for a surprisingly tasty dessert—a perfect way to top off any Mexican meal!

Holiday and Festival Food

Cooking an authentic Mexican holiday meal is a big task for one cook. Typically, the menu includes many courses, and several of the dishes may be elaborate to prepare. Several people usually share the cooking duties in a Mexican kitchen during a holiday. If you're planning to cook for a celebration, you may want to ask for help or limit your menu to one special dish. The recipes that follow here are simplified versions of the traditional foods, but they are still more complicated than the everyday Mexican fare in this book.

Crispy fried buñuelos *topped with cinnamon sugar make for a delicious holiday treat. (See recipe on page 64.)*

Fried Pastry/Buñuelos

This pastry is popular all over Mexico, but it is a special favorite in the state of Oaxaca, located in the south-central part of the country. If you are ever in Oaxaca on Christmas Eve, you can join the local people in eating buñuelos and smashing dishes. With the help of this recipe, you can also enjoy the delicious pastry in your own home.

Pastry ingredients:

4 c. all-purpose flour

2 tbsp. sugar

1 tbsp. baking powder

2 eggs

2 tbsp. milk

¼ c. vegetable oil

1 c. warm water

1 c. vegetable oil (for frying)

Topping ingredients:

½ c. sugar

3 tbsp. cinnamon

1. Thoroughly mix flour, 2 tbsp. sugar, and baking powder in a large bowl.

2. In another bowl, beat together eggs and milk. Then add to dry ingredients. Stir in ¼ c. oil and mix well.

3. Add warm water and mix until dough can be handled easily. (If dough is too dry, add a few more teaspoons of warm water, one at a time.)

4. Place dough on a lightly floured board and knead until smooth.

5. Divide dough into 20 to 24 pieces and shape each into a ball. Flatten balls on the board with the palm of your hand. Cover with a cloth for 20 minutes.

6. On a lightly floured board, use a rolling pin to roll out each flattened ball into a large round shape about 6 or 7 inches in diameter. Let stand for about 5 minutes.

7. Heat 1 c. oil in an electric frying pan* set at 360°F. Just before frying, stretch each buñuelo a little more by hand.

8. Fry each buñuelo until underside is golden brown (about 3 minutes). Using tongs, turn and fry other side until crisp. Remove and drain on a paper towel.

9. In a small bowl, combine ½ c. sugar and 3 tbsp. cinnamon. Sprinkle hot buñuelos with sugar and cinnamon mixture.

Preparation time: 1 hour
Cooking time: 1 hour
Makes 20 to 24

If you don't have an electric frying pan, use a fat thermometer to check the temperature of oil heated in a regular frying pan.

Three Kings Bread/*Rosca de Reyes*

Mexicans make this Christmas treat with a sweet, eggy bread dough. You can speed up preparation by using frozen bread dough, available in the frozen foods section of any grocery store.

2 or 3 loaves frozen bread dough, thawed

1 package candied mixed fruit or candied fruit peel

2 eggs, beaten

3 tbsp. melted butter

½ c. sugar

1. Moisten the ends of the dough loaves and press them together to make a ring. (Make a small ring with two loaves or a bigger ring with three loaves.) Put the ring on a greased cookie sheet.

2. Press the candied fruit into the top of the dough ring in any pattern you like. Set the dough aside in a warm place to rise according to package directions until doubled (about 45 to 60 minutes).

3. Heat the oven to the temperature recommended on the dough package. Brush the top of the ring with the beaten eggs. Bake according to the directions on the dough package.

4. Remove the bread from the oven. Quickly brush the top with the melted butter and sprinkle the sugar over the ring. Return the bread to the oven for 5 minutes.

5. Remove the bread from the oven and set it aside to cool.

Preparation time: 1 to 1½ hours (includes rising time)
Cooking time: 20 to 25 minutes or according to package directions
Makes 1 loaf

Turkey Mole/*Mole de Guajolote*

This recipe cuts down preparation time significantly by using mole paste—a concentrated form of mole sauce that can be mixed with broth or water. Mole paste is available in the Mexican food section of most grocery stores.

1 tbsp. cooking oil

4 serving pieces turkey*

1 to 2 c. turkey or chicken broth

1 9- to 10-oz. jar mole paste

If you prefer a vegetarian mole, you can substitute vegetables such as potatoes, carrots, onions, or peppers for the turkey and vegetable broth for the turkey broth. Even without vegetables, mole sauce is delicious served over rice.

1. Heat the cooking oil in a large, ovenproof pan. Brown the turkey pieces. Cover the pan and put it in the oven at 325°F for 40 to 60 minutes, until the turkey is tender.

2. Remove the turkey pieces to a plate. Pour the pan juices into a large heat-proof measuring cup. Use a turkey baster to remove the fat that floats to the top of the cup.

3. Add enough broth to make 2½ c. of liquid. Pour the liquid back into the pan and add the mole paste. Stir the mixture until all lumps are dissolved.

4. Cook the sauce over medium heat, stirring constantly, until it becomes thick. Use your fingers to shred the turkey into bite-sized pieces. Put the turkey back in the pan and spoon the sauce over them. Lower the heat and cook gently for 10 minutes. Serve the mole with rice.

Preparation time: 25 minutes
Cooking time: 50 to 70 minutes
Serves 4

Index

About the Author

Rosa Coronado began learning about Mexican cooking when she was very young. Her parents, Don Arturo and Doña Elvira Coronado, wanted their daughter to grow up knowing as much as possible about her Mexican heritage. When the Coronados opened La Casa Coronado in Minneapolis, Minnesota, seven-year-old Rosa helped her mother in the restaurant by cleaning chili pods and operating the tortilla machine. When she was fifteen, Rosa created a Christmas dinner all by herself.

After graduating from high school, Coronado attended the University of Mexico in Mexico City. Since that time, she has been involved in the food industry as a restauranteur and a cooking school instructor. Coronado also lectures to many groups about Mexican history and culture. In 1975 Coronado became the first woman admitted to the Geneva Executive Chefs Association, an international organization of chefs and food specialists.

Photo Acknowledgments: The photographs in this book are reproduced courtesy of: © Robert Fried, pp. 2–3; © Louiseanne and Walter Pietrowicz/September 8th Stock, pp. 4 (left), 5 (right), 34, 46, 67, 68; © Robert L. & Diane Wolfe, pp. 4 (right), 5 (left), 6, 18, 33, 37, 42, 45, 48, 51, 52, 56, 61, 62; © Dr. Roma Hoff, p. 10; © David Burckhalter, p. 15; © Nik Wheeler, pp. 16, 26; © H. Huntly Hersch, p. 30.

Cover photos: © Nik Wheeler, front (top); © Walter Pietrowicz/September 8th Stock, front (bottom), spine, back.

The illustrations on pages 7, 19, 27, 29, 31, 32, 35, 38, 39, 41, 43, 47, 53, 54, 57, 63, 65, and 69 and the map on page 8 are by Tim Seeley.